Wise Up President Trump

It's time to confront the Russian Conspiracy scandal head on

William Dunkerley

Published by
Omnicom Press
New Britain, CT, USA
Publishers since 1981

www.OmnicomPress.com

ISBN-13: 978-1979453318
ISBN-10: 1979453314
Printed in the United States of America

Wise Up President Trump is part of the "Russia: Straight Talk on Hushed Issues" monograph series. It is dedicated to the concept of a safe, sustaining, and positive relationship between the United States and the Russian Federation.

A list of other monographs in this series can be found at:

www.OmnicomPress.com/monographs

CONTENTS

Chapter 1
TRUMP FALLS FLAT

Donald Trump is failing to fulfill many promises of his campaign. Who would argue with that? But how could things be turned around for the benefit of the American public?

Take the Russia issue for example. Establishing a positive working relationship was a consistent campaign theme. It apparently resonated with voters.

Elected as president, Trump famously went on to say, "I would love to be able to get along with Russia. Now, you've had a lot of presidents that haven't taken that tack. Look where we are now. Look where we are now."

Chapter 2
TRUMP'S RIGHT

I get his point about Russia. Making an enemy of Russia has yielded no benefit for America.
Instead it's dangerously increased world tension. That's what Trump means, I think, with his "Look where we are now" remark.

But as a result of Trump's mishandling the Russia issue to date, look where HE is now.

Trump, his family, and his associates have been thoroughly vilified by unsubstantiated allegations of an untoward Russia connection. Members of Congress even want to impeach him.

Chapter 3
HIS ENEMIES SCORE

Perpetrators of fraudulent allegations have made great headway. *Variety* magazine reports, "Driven by surges for *The Rachel Maddow Show* and *Last Word with Lawrence O'Donnell*, MSNBC is up a whopping 86 percent in total viewers in primetime compared to second-quarter 2016." I've seen these particular commentators to be two of the most rabid fraudsters in the so-called "Russian Conspiracy."

Trump's primary response? It's been to tweet. But tweets aren't fixing this problem. Trump faces unprincipled opposition pushing a fabricated grand conspiracy. They're playing hardball. But Trump offers softball responses. So far his retaliation has been a bust.

Other than the fabricators, nobody is benefiting

from this. Even principled liberal and progressive opponents are losing out. The Russian Conspiracy is pushing aside everybody's national agenda, liberal or conservative. Trump needs to get serious about this fast.

Chapter 4
TIME FOR HARDBALL

All the fabricators are long overdue for hardball
responses. If Special Counsel Mueller is, as the
Trump side contends, conducting a witch hunt
outside the law, appoint a special prosecutor to
go after him. Don't hint at firing him. Prosecute
him if there is cause. Stop complaining about
Mueller and hold him accountable for any
violations there might be.

If on-air broadcast outlets are using the public
airwaves to perpetrate a fraud on the American
people, call their licenses into question.
Conditions of FCC licenses require that licensees
operate in the public interest. If they are using
their positions of trust to continually lie to the
public, why should they continue to be licensed?

If Hillary Clinton did, as is alleged, commit

crimes, prosecute her and her accomplices. No
more Mr. nice guy.

Fabrications Persist

The fraudsters must be stopped. The story that 17
intelligence agencies found Russian culpability
was proved a hoax. Even the New York Times
admitted that.

Now a group of intelligence experts has proved
forensically that there was no hack in the first
place.

It was a leak from inside.

But yet the fraudulent claims persist in news
reports. Americans have a right to be protected
from massive fraud. The idea is not to silence
divergent viewpoints, but to stop the fraud. This
isn't a matter of one opinion vs. another. It's a
matter of fact vs. fabrication.

Simply correcting the false stories has been
ineffectual so far. This nonsense needs to be
nipped in the bud.

Chapter 5
A FAILED STRATEGY

For years Vladimir Putin handled a multitude of fabricated allegations against him with a softball approach, just like Trump. He never effectively dealt with the problem. Look where HE is now. He's viewed as an international pariah in many quarters.

Allegations include destroying press freedom, blowing up apartment buildings, killing Alexander Litvinenko, invading Crimea. There are no supportive facts. Just allegations. Nonetheless, most people witlessly believe the apparent nonsense.

I've written four books documenting the fabrications. Taken together, the accusations represent an attempt by Putin's political enemies to take him down.

That's what Trump's political enemies are doing to him. The Russian Conspiracy isn't the real issue. It's just another effort by political enemies to take down Trump. It's not Russia. It's an attempted take down.

Chapter 6
THE US SET THE NORM

You know, even if the Russian Conspiracy allegations were true, what's the big deal? Russia would still be well within international norms the United States established through its own actions.

Trump has allowed himself to be baited into a defensive posture over a nonsense issue.

He faces a Congress that itself has fraudsters in its midst. They're trying to use Russia in their efforts to get rid of him.

The rest of Congress, unfortunately, is mostly full of members who have been duped by long-running false and mythical stories about Russia.

Chapter 7
TRUMP'S SURRENDER

Now in late 2017 it looks like Trump is trying to appease the dupsters by compromising his promise of a positive working relationship with Russia.

But he should think of his own words, "Look where we are now." If he doesn't stick to his promise we will find ourselves STUCK where we are now. Or worse.

The only way out for Trump I see is to use full force to take on the Russia myth and the fraudsters that are using it to destroy his presidency no matter how much damage is done to the country.

It's time to wise up to that, President Trump.

Chapter 8
CHARLOTTESVILLE

The Charlottesville nazi incident of late August 2017 took the spotlight away from the Russian Conspiracy allegations. But the Charlottesville story, as I see it, is just another component of the ongoing efforts to unseat Trump, no matter what damage is done to the country.

First there was the campaign to defeat him in the Electoral College. When that failed, Trump's enemies attempted to get Congress to reject the Electoral College vote. Then they tried to lay the grounds for impeachment on the basis of alleged criminal connections with Russia. That effort is ongoing. Meanwhile there was also a failed attempt to invoke the 25th Amendment of the Constitution to throw him out on the basis of insanity. There may be another attempt at that forthcoming.

The media gives extensive coverage to all the take-down attempts. Trump's enemies couch the accusations as black-and-white issues. That makes them easier for audiences to understand and for media outlets to cover.

Chapter 9
DISECTING ALL THIS

The Charlottesville campaign seems aimed at weakening Trump by characterizing him as a nazi sympathizer or enabler. That's the real story here, I think.

Looking critically at what actually happened in Charlottesville, I see two main aspects. The first is the vehicular assault on a crowd that killed someone. The second is the motive behind those responsible for that assault and the overall level of violence.

Comparisons

In May 2017 there was another vehicular assault, that time in Times Square. Someone was killed there too. It was a big story, but not nearly as big as Charlottesville.

CNN continued to report on the Charlottesville incident non-stop all through the first night. There were no new developments to report on. Primarily it was a rant against Trump, peppered with the few facts known about Charlottesville.

Unlike Charlottesville, the New York perpetrator apparently had no political motive. But we've seen other deaths motivated by political ideology in the past. The 2009 Fort Hood massacre comes to mind. Thirteen people were killed there.

The Charlottesville and Fort Hood stories both included media and political commentary on how the then sitting president reacted.

In the case of Trump, his first words were to condemn the whole incident unequivocally. One could observe him reading his statement. At one point he seems to have gone off script and added that he thought there was culpability for the violence on multiple sides. As can be observed in video of the incident, his claim is irrefutably verifiable.

Trump was criticized for not calling out the nazi-type groups by name. Shortly thereafter he did, but many continued their condemnation of Trump. And when he continued his criticism of multiple sides for the violence at his Trump

Tower press event, he reinvigorated his critics.

After the Fort Hood incident, Obama's first words were to say "I want to just assure all of us that we're going to get to the bottom of exactly what happened." Much later his administration finally labeled it a case of workplace violence, despite the shooter's radical Islamic bent. It wasn't until six years later that Obama compared the shooting to other domestic terror events. I'm not sure that he is yet to specifically label Fort Hood as an act of terrorism plain and simple.

While Obama was criticized by Republicans for his descriptions of Fort Hood, it never rose to the level of what's going on now vis-a-vis Charlottesville.

Harmful Campaign

There are two very sad aspects to this campaign against Trump. The first is the gullibility and susceptibility to manipulation of the news consumers. The second is the inability of Trump to effectively handle the dirty tactics that are being used against him. He's helpless in fighting this trumped up allegation. I'm not offering partisan support for Trump. But I think the long-running vicious campaign against him does far greater harm to the country than Trump's loose-canon approach to governance.

There's another sleight of hand going on in this political attack on Trump. His enemies claim Trump has proclaimed a moral equivalency between the nazi protestors and the anti-nazi ones. He said no such thing. He didn't address that matter at all. What he did say is that he saw shared culpability for the violence, that's all. But I haven't seen that the Trump team is skillful enough to call them out on this effectively.

Charlottesville aside, the Russian Conspiracy remains an ongoing attempt to neutralize the result of our last presidential election. Surprisingly there is much ammunition that can be used to decimate the case perpetrators are making. It clearly could be neutralized, if done right. But the Trump team shows no sign of doing it right.

Again, it's time to wise up to all this, President Trump.

Appendix I
THE AUTHOR

William Dunkerley is a media business analyst and Senior Fellow at American University in Moscow. He has worked on behalf of US interests in promoting press freedom in Eastern Europe and the former Soviet Union. He was commissioned by the International Federation of Journalists to analyze problems in certain Western press coverage of Russian issues. Mr. Dunkerley has been instrumental in shaping laws governing the media in Eastern Europe and Russia and has offered testimony to the United States Congress on media concerns. He has personally done intensive work in seven post communist countries, including interventions in seventeen different cities across all Russia. He is principal of William Dunkerley Publishing Consultants, and publisher of two industry monthlies, *Editors Only* and the *STRAT* newsletter.

THIS SERIES

"Russia: Straight Talk on Hushed Issues" is a monograph series that looks behind the popular headlines and presents iconoclastic analyses. The books explain aspects of mainstream news that are either being distorted, glossed over, or hushed up.

The etiology of these media distortions is complex. Historically there was little harshness in the coverage of Yeltsin's misdeeds, perhaps a result of Western giddiness over the collapse of the Soviet Union.

When Putin entered the scene in 1999 the kid gloves came off. He was demonized. Russian tycoons who had been involved in skullduggery under Yeltsin found the new leader problematic.

Boris Berezovsky, one of the tycoons, carried

media attacks to new heights after fleeing to London in 2001 to evade corruption charges. He packaged and distributed highly engaging news stories with associated graphics and interview opportunities to media outlets worldwide. Probably because of that convenience, they were readily accepted by the media unquestioningly despite their lack of factual bases.

Inexplicably, after Berezovsky's 2014 death, the stream of demonizing stories continued. Had Berezovsky's campaign just made an indelible impression that still taints the views of media and political leaders in the US and elsewhere? Or is there a new kingpin yet to be identified?

Regardless, many people have indeed formed beliefs based on the prevalence of distorted news and are committed to them. It would be unrealistic to think many of these folks will accept any contravening facts and analyses.

So the intention of this series is to give open-minded audiences in the US and other Western countries insights into misleading and fabricated reportage. That should allow them to arrive at more realistic and fact-based understandings, thus facilitating their serving more responsibly as members of our society. The intention is not to exonerate anyone who has been accused, but to point out that the accusers are liars and fabricators. (Note: Monographs in this series appear in no particular order.)

H.G. Wells once said: "Civilization is in a race between education and catastrophe."

But what is now unfolding in the theater of US-Russia relations is a race between catastrophe and utter disaster.

One entrant is the United States, and the other is Russia. Which country is on which side actually makes no difference. In this race, there are allegations, then sanctions, and then retributions for the previous actions. It is a self perpetuating loop.

This is a race in which the winner will personify either political buffoonery or plain stupidity. And which of the two is the victor will also make no difference. The main point for the rest of us is that this race will cause us all to lose.

As part of the "Russia: Straight Talk on Hushed Issues" monograph series, this book is dedicated to ending that foolish race, and to the concept of a safe, sustaining, and positive relationship between the United States and the Russian Federation.

Appendix III
ACKNOWLEDGMENT

In the face of much media misinformation about Russia, I wish to acknowledge the effort and perseverance of all who have spoken and written the honest truth. They have shown great courage in bucking the unfortunate mainstream trend toward fabrication. Their work serves as an essential predicate to this book. --W.D.